Contents

A strange beast

Slow, heavy footsteps move
through the forest. Crack!
Giant claws break a branch.
A big ground sloth chomps
on the leaves.

ICE AGE ANIMALS

Pebble® Plus

Ground Sloths

by Joy Frisch-Schmoll

Consulting Editor: Gail Saunders-Smith, PhD

Content Consultant: Margaret M. Yacobucci, PhD
Education and Outreach Coordinator,
Paleontological Society; Associate Professor,
Department of Geology, Bowling Green State University

Raintree is an imprint of Capstone Global Library Limited, a company incorporated in England and Wales having its registered office at 7 Pilgrim Street, London, EC4V 6LB – Registered company number: 6695582

www.raintree.co.uk
myorders@raintree.co.uk

Editorial Credits
Jeni Wittrock, editor; Peggie Carley and Janet Kusmierski, designers; Wanda Winch, media researcher; Laura Manthe, production specialist

ISBN 978 1 4062 9366 1 (hardback)
18 17 16 15 14
10 9 8 7 6 5 4 3 2 1

ISBN 978 1 4062 9373 9 (paperback)
19 18 17 16
10 9 8 7 6 5 4 3 2 1

British Library Cataloguing in Publication Data
A full catalogue record for this book is available from the British Library.

Photo Credits
Illustrator: Jon Hughes
Shutterstock: Alex Staroseltsev, snowball, April Cat, icicles, Leigh Prather, ice crystals, LilKar, cover background, pcruciatti, interior background

Printed and bound in China.

About 35,000 years ago,
ground sloths roamed the land.
Some were the size of black
bears. Others were as big
as elephants!

Ground level

Ground sloths lived in North and South America during the Ice Age. They made their homes in caves, grasslands and forests.

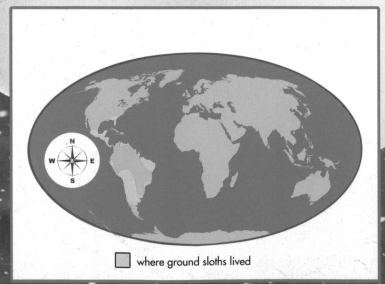

where ground sloths lived

Too big to climb trees, ground sloths lived on the ground. They walked on all fours with their clawed feet turned inwards.

Big and strong

Ground sloths had shaggy fur and sharp claws. They stood on strong back legs to reach the leafy treetops. Thick tails helped them to balance.

Along with leaves, sloths ate twigs and grasses. Their powerful jaws and flat teeth were good for grinding up plants.

Gentle giants

Ground sloths lived on their own. Sloths were slow and gentle. But if a sloth was attacked, it would fight back.

A fighting ground sloth stood up to look bigger. Swipe! It swung its front claws at predators such as the sabretooth cat.

About 10,000 years ago, Earth changed. The planet warmed. Human hunters moved in. With less food and more predators, ground sloths became extinct.

Glossary

claw hard, curved nail on the foot of an animal

extinct no longer living; an extinct animal is one that has died out, with no more of its kind

grassland large, open area where grass and low plants grow

Ice Age time when much of Earth was covered in ice; the last ice age ended about 11,500 years ago

jaw part of the mouth used to grab, bite and chew

predator animal that hunts other animals for food

Read more

First Encyclopedia of Dinosaurs and Prehistoric Life
(Usborne First Encyclopedias), Sam Taplin (Usborne
Publishing Ltd, 2011)

Ice Age Giants (Wild Age), Steve Parker
(QEB Publishing, 2011)

The Ice Age Tracker's Guide, Adrian Lister and Martin
Ursell (Frances Lincoln Children's Books, 2010)

Websites

www.bbc.co.uk/nature/life/Megatheriidae
Did you know that a ground sloth's claws could be
50 centimetres long? Learn more fascinating facts
about this giant creature!

www.nhm.ac.uk/kids-only/dinosaurs/
Find out everything you need to know about
prehistoric life. Look at 3-D dinosaurs, learn fun
facts, play games and take a quiz!

Index